Vegan Keto Cookbook

Take your Vegan Cooking on the Next Level! Quick & Simple Vegan Recipes to Satisfy your Cravings Healthily and Losing Weight Rapidly

Written By

JANE BRACE

Table of Contents

ANY BERRY PIE 52

TARTE TATIN 54

CHOCOLATE SILK PIE 56

SKY-HIGH PEANUT BUTTER PIE 58

PECAN PIE 60

NEW YORK–STYLE CHEESECAKE 64

PISTACHIO ROSE CHEESECAKE 66

CARAMEL CHAI CHEESECAKE 68

PUMPKIN PECAN CHEESECAKE 71

CHOCOLATE BROWNIE CHEESECAKE 73

CHOCOLATE PISTACHIO TART 77

PEARBERRY TART 79

ALMOND APPLE TART 81

CRANBERRY WHITE CHOCOLATE CITRUS TART 83

WHITE CHOCOLATE PEANUT BUTTER PRETZEL TARTLETS 85

PEACHY KEEN COBBLER 87

CHERRY CLAFOUTIS 89

APPLE CRISP 91

MILLE-FEUILLE 92

MINI MAPLE DONUTS 94

BELGIAN WAFFLES 96

BARS

CHERRY ALMOND BISCOTTI

YIELD: 20 BISCOTTI

This tart and slightly sweet cookie complements tea or coffee beautifully with its fruity notes. Not only is it pleasing to the taste buds, your eyes are in for a treat with deep red cherries studded throughout.

2 tablespoons flaxseed meal

4 tablespoons water

⅓ cup non dairy margarine

¾ cup sugar

1½ teaspoons almond extract

½ teaspoon salt

2 teaspoons baking powder

1 cup sorghum flour

¾ cup brown rice flour

½ cup potato starch

1 teaspoon xanthan gum

¼ cup non dairy milk

1 cup dried cherries

- Preheat oven to 325°F. Combine the flaxseed meal and water into a bowl and let rest for 5 minutes, until gelled.

- In a large bowl, cream together the margarine and sugar until smooth. Add the prepared flaxseed meal, almond extract, and salt.

11

- In a separate bowl, whisk together the baking powder, sorghum flour, brown rice flour, potato starch, and xanthan gum. Gradually incorporate into the sugar mixture. Add non dairy milk, 1 tablespoon at a time, until a soft dough forms. It should be just dry enough to handle and shape into two balls. Add a touch more sorghum flour or milk to create the right consistency. The dough shouldn't crumble apart, but it also shouldn't be too sticky. Fold in the dried cherries until even distributed.

- Directly on an ungreased cookie sheet, shape the cookie dough into two ovals, about 2.5 inches wide and 1.25 inches tall. Bake in preheated oven for about 30 minutes, until lightly golden on edges. Let cool and then slice cookies diagonally. Place freshly cut cookies on their sides and bake an additional 8 minutes. Turn cookies over and bake another 8 minutes. And one more time … flip, and bake a final 8 minutes. Let cool completely before enjoying. Store in airtight container for up to 3 weeks.

MARBLE BISCOTTI

YIELD: 18 BISCOTTI

Chocolate and vanilla mingle in this delightful-looking cookie. Dip into piping hot coffee or hot chocolate for the ultimate biscotti experience. If you're sharing, these make great gifts once you wrap them up in shiny plastic wrap and adorn them with a bow, especially when paired with your favorite blend of coffee.

3 tablespoons flaxseed meal

6 tablespoons water

½ cup sugar

½ cup non dairy margarine

½ teaspoon vanilla extract

1 cup sorghum flour

¾ cup brown rice flour

½ cup potato starch

¼ cup tapioca flour

1 teaspoon xanthan gum

1½ teaspoons baking powder

½ teaspoon salt

½ cup non dairy chocolate chips, melted, plus 1 cup chocolate chips, melted, for drizzling

- Preheat oven to 325°F.

- In a small bowl, combine flaxseed meal with water and let rest until gelled, for about 5 minutes. In large mixing bowl, cream together the sugar and the

13

margarine. Add the prepared flaxseed meal and vanilla extract and mix well. In a separate bowl, combine the sorghum flour, brown rice flour, potato starch, tapioca flour, xanthan gum, baking powder, and salt. Stir well to evenly incorporate.

- Slowly combine the flour mixture with the margarine mixture until clumpy. Divide dough into two sections, leaving half in the mixing bowl and setting the rest aside. Gently stir in the ½ cup melted chocolate chips with one-half of the dough until very well combined, scraping bowl as needed.

- Now you will have two sections of dough: one chocolate and one vanilla. Shape the vanilla dough into two balls. Shape the chocolate mixture into two balls as well. Then, roll each section into long ropes, so that you have four long ropes of both chocolate and vanilla—about 10 inches long each.

- Working on an ungreased baking sheet, place one chocolate rope and one vanilla rope side by side and then twist over one another, pressing together to form a flat log about 3 inches by 10 inches and then repeat with other two ropes.

- Bake for 28 minutes, until lightly golden brown on edges, and then remove from the oven and place onto a wire rack to let completely cool. Using a serrated knife, slice diagonally into 3 × 1-inch cookies and place freshly cut cookies on their sides on the cookie sheet.

- Bake cookies for 10 minutes. Flip and bake for 10 more minutes. Flip one more time and bake for 5 more minutes. Let cool completely and then drizzle or coat one side with melted chocolate.

- Store in airtight container for up to 1 month.

ULTIMATE FUDGY BROWNIES

YIELD: 12 BROWNIES

These brownies boast a crispy, flaky, paper-thin layer atop a chewy, gooey perfect square of brownie bliss. Even though these brownies are pretty delicious all by their lonesome, they do take kindly to a thin layer of frosting on top, too. Try them topped with Fluffy Chocolate Frosting or Caramel Frosting for an extra- indulgent treat!

¾ cup superfine brown rice flour

¼ cup almond meal

¼ cup potato starch

¼ cup sorghum flour

1 teaspoon xanthan gum

½ teaspoon baking soda

1 teaspoon salt

3 cups chopped non dairy chocolate or chocolate chips

1 cup sugar

¼ cup non dairy margarine

½ cup strong coffee

2 tablespoons ground chia seed mixed with 5 tablespoons hot water

1 teaspoon vanilla extract

1 cup non dairy white chocolate chips (optional)

- Preheat oven 325°F and lightly grease a 9 × 13-inch metal pan.

- In a large electric mixing bowl, whisk together the superfine brown rice flour, almond meal, potato starch, sorghum flour, xanthan gum, baking soda, and salt.

- Place the chocolate chips into a large heat-safe bowl.

- In a 2-quart saucepan over medium heat, combine the sugar, margarine, and ¼ cup of the coffee and bring to a boil, stirring often. Once boiling, immediately remove from the heat and pour the hot sugar mixture directly onto the chocolate chips, stirring quickly to combine thoroughly. Transfer to the mixing bowl containing the flour mixture along with the prepared chia gel and vanilla extract and mix on medium-high speed until smooth. Add in the additional ¼ cup coffee and mix well. If you're using them, fold in white chocolate chips.

- Spread the batter in the prepared baking pan—the batter will be tacky. Bake for 45 to 50 minutes. Let cool completely before cutting into squares and serving. Store in airtight container for up to 3 days.

BLONDIES

YIELD: 12 BLONDIES

Blondies are lighter than brownies in taste, texture, and color but still bear a delicious resemblance to their chocolate pals. Try these topped with Peanut Butter Banana Ice Cream.

2 tablespoons flaxseed meal

4 tablespoons water

⅓ cup coconut palm sugar

1 teaspoon vanilla extract

1 cup brown rice flour

½ cup almond meal

¼ cup potato starch

1 teaspoon xanthan gum

½ teaspoon salt

½ cup non dairy margarine

1 tablespoon coconut oil

1½ cups non dairy white chocolate chips or pieces

½ cup non dairy mini chocolate chips

- Preheat oven to 350°F. Lightly grease an 8 × 8-inch baking pan.

- In a small bowl, combine the flaxseed meal and water and let rest until gelled,

18

for about 5 minutes. Stir in the coconut palm sugar and vanilla extract. In a separate bowl, whisk together the brown rice flour, almond meal, potato starch, xanthan gum, and salt.

- Over a double boiler, on medium-low heat, melt the margarine, coconut oil, and white chocolate until smooth. Remove from heat. Stir white chocolate mixture into the flour mixture along with the flaxseed meal mixture until a batter forms. Fold in the mini chocolate chips. Press the batter into the prepared baking pan and bake for 27 minutes, or until golden brown on edges. Let cool completely, for at least 2 hours, before serving. Store in airtight container for up to 1 week.

LIGHTEN UP LEMON BARS

YIELD: 16 BARS

These are a lightened-up version of traditional lemon bars, leaving out the eggs and butter and opting for plant-based ingredients instead. Agar can easily be sourced at local health food stores or Asian markets. If you can only source agar bars or flakes, simply run them through a spice grinder until powdered.

CRUST

2 tablespoons flaxseed meal

4 tablespoons water

1½ cups almond meal

¼ teaspoon salt

3 tablespoons sugar

FILLING

2 cups water

1½ tablespoons agar powder

1¼ cups sugar

1 cup freshly squeezed lemon juice (about 6 lemons' worth)

1 drop natural yellow food coloring

¼ cup cornstarch dissolved completely in ¼ cup water

Confectioner's sugar, for dusting

• Preheat oven to 400°F.

- In a small bowl, mix the flaxseed meal with the water until gelled, for about 5 minutes. In a medium bowl, whisk together the rest of the crust ingredients and then massage the prepared flaxseed meal into the almond meal mixture until well blended. Press crust into a lightly greased 8 × 8- inch baking pan. Bake for 12 to 15 minutes, until golden brown on edges. Remove from oven and let cool while you make the filling.

- To make the filling, bring the 2 cups water and agar powder to a boil over medium heat, stirring constantly with a whisk. Let boil for 3 to 5 minutes, until thickened and all agar has dissolved. (Be sure that all agar has dissolved or your lemon bars won't set correctly.) Stir in the sugar, lemon juice, food coloring, and cornstarch slurry. Continue to cook over medium heat, bringing back up to a boil. Let boil for about 3 minutes, until thickened. Pour the mixture on top of the crust and chill immediately on a flat surface in your refrigerator. Chill 2 hours, or until firm. Cut into squares. Dust with confectioners sugar before serving. Store in refrigerator for up to 1 week.

BLUEBERRY BARS

YIELD: 16 BARS

These delicious bars are similar to boxed cereal bars, only tastier and without any added preservatives or chemicals! If blueberry's not your favorite, feel free to use any other type of preserves for endless flavor variations.

1½ cups pecans

1½ cups sorghum flour, plus more as needed for rolling and shaping

⅓ cup potato starch

1 teaspoon baking powder

1 teaspoon xanthan gum

¾ cup non dairy margarine

1 cup sugar

2 tablespoons flaxseed meal

4 tablespoons water

1 cup high-quality blueberry preserves

- Preheat oven to 400°F. Lightly grease and flour the bottom and sides of an 8 × 8-inch baking pan.

- Lay pecans in an even layer on a standard cookie sheet so that they do not overlap. Toast pecans for about 10 minutes, or until fragrant and flavorful. Watch carefully so that they do not burn. Once toasted, remove from cookie sheet and set aside until cool. Toss the toasted pecans into a food processor and pulse just until crumbly. Don't overmix.

- In a medium bowl, sift together sorghum flour, potato starch, baking powder, and xanthan gum. Stir in the pulsed pecans.

- In a separate mixing bowl, cream together the margarine and sugar until smooth.

- In a small bowl, combine the flaxseed meal with the water and let rest until gelled, for about 5 minutes. Fold in prepared flaxseed meal with the margarine mixture and mix until combined. Gradually add in the flour mixture, adding up to ⅓ cup additional sorghum flour until the dough can be easily handled. Shape into two separate disks and chill until cold.

- Once the dough is well chilled, take one of the disks and place it in between two pieces of parchment paper and roll until large enough to cover the baking pan.

- Transfer the dough to cover the bottom of the pan, gently pushing down the edges to form a wall around the crust. Spread the blueberry preserves evenly over the layer of crust.

- Take the second disk of dough and crumble into small pieces. Top the jam liberally with dough crumbles. Chill the pan in your freezer while you preheat oven to 350°F.

- Bake for about 35 minutes or until crust becomes golden brown.

- Let cool, then slice into squares. Store bars in an airtight container in refrigerator for up to 1 week.

PEANUT BUTTER MAPLE CRISPY TREATS

YIELD: 12 BARS

I never tire of crispy rice treats. These feature peanut butter and are lightly painted with melted chocolate to give them extra oomph! Try these with chocolate hazelnut butter (Justin's is a great choice) instead of peanut butter. Then just try not to eat the whole pan yourself.

3 tablespoons coconut oil

4 cups vegan marshmallows, such as Dandies

1 teaspoon maple extract

2 tablespoons maple syrup

½ cup smooth peanut butter

6 cups gluten-free crispy rice cereal

1 cup non dairy chocolate chips

- Lightly grease an 8 × 8-inch baking dish using either margarine or coconut oil.

- In a large saucepan over medium heat, melt the 3 tablespoons coconut oil slightly so that the bottom of the saucepan is coated. Add the marshmallows and heat over medium heat until mostly melted, stirring often to prevent burning. Stir in the maple extract, maple syrup, and peanut butter and continue to stir until completely incorporated.

- Place crispy rice cereal into a large bowl and pour hot marshmallow mixture over the crispy rice cereal. Mix quickly to ensure that all the cereal is coated with marshmallow mixture. Spread mixture into the prepared pan and press down firmly using greased hands. Let set until hardened, for about 2 hours. Cut into 2 × 2-inch squares.

- Melt chocolate over double boiler and drizzle the chocolate onto all sides of the bars and place onto waxed paper or a silicone mat. Let chocolate harden completely before enjoying. Store in airtight container for up to 1 week.

TOFFEE CRACKER COOKIES

YIELD: 24 COOKIES

Utilizing crunchy crackers, these cookie bars have a salty and sweet flavor with a candy-like crunch. Out of crackers? You can also use plain cookies to make these; opt for a crunchy cookie such as vanilla wafers or graham crackers.

4 to 5 ounces (about 25 crackers) gluten-free, egg-free crackers, such as Glutino's table crackers

½ cup non dairy margarine

½ cup brown sugar

1 cup semi-sweet non dairy chocolate chips

½ cup sliced toasted almonds or pecans

- Preheat oven to 400°F. Line a medium (about 9 × 13 inches) lipped cookie sheet or baking pan with parchment paper.

- Arrange the crackers on the parchment, as best as you can, in a single layer. Small gaps in between are fine.

- In a 2-quart saucepan, bring together the margarine and brown sugar over medium heat. Stir often, and bring to a boil. Once it hits a boil, let cook for 3 minutes, without stirring. Carefully and strategically pour the hot candy syrup over the crackers to cover. Bake for 5 minutes. Immediately remove from the oven and sprinkle the chocolate chips to cover. Let set for about 4 minutes, and then spread the chocolate to evenly cover the candy. Sprinkle with the almonds. Let rest for 1 hour in a cool place. Freeze briefly until candy has hardened and then cut into squares. Store in airtight container for up to 1 week.

LUSCIOUS PIES, PASTRIES, TARTS, AND CHEESECAKES

Baking pies is a wonderful hobby because with just a little bit of extra effort, you end up with a dessert that is so impressive it just begs to be shared. I recommend not trying to bake pies that use the Flakey Classic Pie Crust or Puff Pastry on especially humid days, as the tendency for the dough to stick will be much greater, resulting in a frustrating pie baking experience. Shoot for cooler or dry summer days instead for perfect pies every time.

BASICS

FLAKEY CLASSIC PIE CRUST

YIELD: 2 STANDARD-SIZE PIE CRUSTS, OR ENOUGH FOR 1 LATTICE-TOPPED OR COVERED PIE

This piecrust is a staple in this chapter. With a flaky, buttery consistency, it truly does make a pie stand out!

1 cup superfine brown rice flour

¾ cup white rice flour

½ cup potato starch

½ cup tapioca flour

1½ teaspoons xanthan gum

½ teaspoon baking powder

3 tablespoons sugar

10 tablespoons cold non dairy margarine

3 tablespoons lemon juice

½ cup ice-cold water

- In a large bowl, whisk together the superfine brown rice flour, white rice flour, potato starch, tapioca flour, xanthan gum, baking powder, and sugar.

- Drop the margarine into the flour mixture by tablespoons. Use fingers or pastry blender to quickly mix into an even crumble. Using a large fork, stir in the lemon juice and cold water until a soft dough forms. If the dough seems too sticky, add a touch more brown rice flour. Wrap in plastic wrap and chill in the freezer for 15 minutes, or refrigerator for at least 1 hour before using.

- Keeps tightly covered in refrigerator for up to 1 week, and frozen for up to 3 months.

This crust freezes well, so feel free to shape the unbaked dough into a patty and place into two freezer- safe bags (double layered), and, the day before using, allow to thaw in refrigerator overnight before rolling out to use in a recipe. Or roll it out onto two aluminum pie pans, cover in plastic wrap, and freeze. Pie makin' is easy if you already have the crusts prepared ahead of time!

PUFF PASTRY

YIELD: 20 SERVINGS

The key to this super-flakey pastry is keeping the dough cold! Be sure to chill adequately between rotations to ensure a workable dough. I also recommend chilling all ingredients before getting started.

¾ cup superfine brown rice flour

¾ cup white rice flour

⅔ cup potato starch

⅓ cup tapioca flour

2 teaspoons xanthan gum

1¼ cups very cold non dairy margarine

½ cup ice-cold water

- In a large bowl, whisk together the brown rice flour, ½ cup of the white rice flour, potato starch, tapioca flour, and xanthan gum. Drop in the margarine by the spoonful. Using clean hands, quickly cut the margarine into the flour until the mixture resembles pebbles.

- Add in the cold water and mix quickly to form a slightly sticky dough. Punch down into the bowl to flatten the dough and sprinkle with 2 tablespoons white rice flour; pat into the dough to make it less sticky. Flip and repeat with the additional 2 tablespoons white rice flour.

- Chill the dough for 20 minutes in the freezer.

- In between two sheets of parchment paper, roll out the dough into a rectangle about 5 × 9 inches. Use a straight edge to square up the edges, forming a solid rectangle. Work quickly so that the dough stays cold!

- Fold the dough into thirds (like folding a letter) and rotate a quarter of a turn. Use the parchment to help fold the dough over evenly. Roll it out again into another rectangle 5 × 9 inches. Fold it into thirds once again. Wrap loosely in parchment and chill in the freezer for an additional 20 minutes.

- Repeat the steps again, exactly as described above. Wrap and chill the puff pastry until ready to use. When working with the pastry, be sure not to roll it out too thin, ⅓ to ½ of an inch is just right.

- Use as directed in recipes calling for puff pastry. To deepen the color of the pastry, mix 2 teaspoons cornstarch with ½ cup water—bring to a boil over medium heat and cook until translucent. Brush a little of the paste onto the surface before baking. Keeps frozen for up to 1 month.

EASY PUFF COOKIES

Preheat oven to 400°F. Dust a sheet of parchment with turbinado sugar. Place the puff pastry dough onto the sugared surface and dust with more sugar. Place another sheet of parchment onto the dough and roll out to ⅓ to ½ inch thick. Use a fun cookie cutter to cut out shapes.

Bake on a parchment-covered cookie sheet for about 20 minutes, until golden brown.

PIES

SUGAR CRUNCH APPLE PIE

YIELD: 8 SERVINGS

Adding the sugary syrup to the assembled pie is fun and delicious, as it creates a crisp sugar topping, not unlike the candy crunch from crème brûlée.

1 recipe <u>Flakey Classic Piecrust</u>

APPLES

8 medium Granny Smith apples

½ teaspoon cardamom

1 teaspoon cinnamon

½ teaspoon cloves

SAUCE

½ cup non dairy margarine

4 tablespoons superfine brown rice flour

¼ cup water

1 cup packed brown sugar

- Prepare the pie dough according to recipe directions, divide into two disks and chill for 2 hours in your refrigerator. Core and peel the apples. Slice thinly and lightly toss with cardamom, cinnamon, and cloves.

- Once pie crusts are chilled, roll out one section of dough in between two sheets of parchment paper to a ¼ inch thickness. Use the parchment paper to help flip the rolled out crust into a lightly greased pie pan. Cut off excess dough and reserve.

- Heap the sliced apples into a mound on top of the crust in the pie pan.

- Take the second chilled dough disk and roll to same thickness in between two sheets of parchment paper. As you did with the first crust, use the parchment to help you flip the dough over on top of the mound of apples. If any dough rips, simply use your fingertips dipped in water to help seal it back together. Build up the sides with excess dough to form a shallow wall as the outer crust. Make a few ¼-inch-wide slits in the top crust to vent.

- Whisk the ingredients for the sauce together into a 2-quart saucepan on medium heat and let it come to a boil, while stirring occasionally. After it has come to a boil, reduce heat to simmer and let cook for 2 minutes. Remove the sauce from the heat.

- Preheat your oven to 425°F. Pour the sugar mixture on top of pie crust, aiming mostly for the slits in the center, and allow any excess to drip over sides. Once all sauce has been added to the pie use a pastry brush to gently brush the remaining syrup evenly over the pie.

- Bake for 15 minutes, then reduce oven temp to 350°F and bake for an additional 35 to 45 minutes. Remove from oven, and let cool for at least 2 hours before serving. Store in airtight container for up to 2 days.

BANANA CREAM PIE

YIELD: 10 SERVINGS

Up until the Great Depression, bananas were practically unheard of in desserts. Apparently, it was the frugalness of using the overripe bananas that led to incorporating them into sweets. With its rich, cream filling, this pie is the very opposite of frugal! It is best enjoyed right after cooling as the bananas tend to discolor after a day or so; one very good way to remedy this is to freeze the pie immediately after it cools and serve mostly frozen.

½ recipe <u>Flakey Classic Pie Crust</u>

FILLING

¾ cup sugar

⅓ cup white rice flour

¼ teaspoon salt

2 cups non dairy milk

3 tablespoons cornstarch mixed with 3 tablespoons water

2 tablespoons non dairy margarine

2 teaspoons vanilla extract

4 large bananas

- Preheat oven to 400°F.

- Prepare the pie crust according to recipe directions and then blind bake in

41

oven for 10 minutes. Reduce oven temperature to 350°F.

- In a 2-quart saucepan, whisk together the sugar, white rice flour, salt, nondairy milk, and cornstarch slurry. Add the margarine and vanilla extract. Heat over medium heat until the mixture comes to a boil, stirring constantly. Let cook for 1 minute, still stirring constantly, until the mixture thickens considerably.

- Slice the bananas into the baked pie crust forming an even layer. Pour the hot sugar mixture over the bananas to cover and bake in preheated oven for 15 minutes. Remove from oven and let cool. Chill and serve with fresh banana slices and Sweetened Whipped Coconut Cream. Store in airtight container in refrigerator for up to 2 days.

KEY LIME PIE

YIELD: 10 SERVINGS

Sweet yet sour, this creamy pie will transport you straight to the Florida Keys. I recommend using bottled key lime juice for ease and availability.

CRUST

1 cup gluten-free cookie crumbs (use hard cookie such as Pizzelles, Cinnamon Graham Crackers, Vanilla Wafers, etc.)

1 cup ground pecans

3 tablespoons sugar

2 tablespoons ground chia seed mixed with 4 tablespoons water

1 tablespoon coconut oil

FILLING

1 (350 g) package extra-firm silken tofu

1 cup key lime juice

1 cup canned full-fat coconut milk

½ cup coconut cream from the top of a can of full-fat coconut milk

1 cup sugar

2 tablespoons confectioners sugar

¾ teaspoons salt

¼ cup besan/chickpea flour

¼ cup white rice flour

2 tablespoons cornstarch

1 teaspoon lime zest, plus more for topping

- Preheat oven to 375°F.

- Mix together all the crust ingredients, in order given, and press into a standard-size pie pan.

- In the bowl of a food processor, place the filling ingredients, pulsing a few times after each addition, until smooth. Be sure to scrape down sides as needed.

- Pour the filling mixture into the crust and carefully transfer to the middle rack of your oven. Bake for 20 minutes. Reduce heat to 300°F and bake for an additional 40 to 45 minutes, until very lightly golden brown on edges. Let cool at room temperature and then chill in refrigerator overnight. Top with lime zest and Sweetened Whipped Coconut Cream. Store in airtight container in refrigerator for up to 2 days.

ALLERGY NOTE

If you have a nut allergy and would like to make this pie, simply swap out the pecans in the crust for toasted sunflower or pumpkin seeds.

PUMPKIN PIE

YIELD: 10 SERVINGS

Popular during the autumn months, pumpkin pie didn't become the traditional dessert of Thanksgiving until the early 1800s. This pumpkin pie is just like the ones my mother used to make for the holiday—with a crust that's softer on the bottom and crispy on the sides. Strange as it sounds, that was always my favorite part of the pie!

½ recipe <u>Flakey Classic Pie Crust</u>

1 cup sugar

1 teaspoon cinnamon

1 teaspoon ginger

½ teaspoon ground cloves

¼ teaspoon ground nutmeg

1 teaspoon salt

1 (350 g) package extra-firm silken tofu

1½ teaspoons vanilla extract

⅓ cup superfine brown rice flour

2 cups canned pumpkin puree

¼ cup apple cider or nondairy milk

- Prepare the pie crust according to recipe directions. Shape the dough into a disk and chill in the refrigerator for at least 1 hour.

- Preheat oven to 425°F. Roll out the crust in between two pieces of parchment and then flip over to lay the pie crust evenly into the bottom of a standard-size pie pan. Pinch the top to make the pie fancy, or flute.

- Combine all the ingredients for the pie filling in a food processor and blend until very smooth. Spread pie filling into unbaked crust and bake for 15 minutes.

- Reduce your oven temperature to 350°F and bake for an additional 40 minutes, or until the crust is golden brown. Let pie cool completely and refrigerate for at least 4 hours before serving. This pie is best when chilled overnight. Store in airtight container in refrigerator for up to 5 days.

STRAWBERRY PIE

YIELD: 10 SERVINGS

Strawberry Pie always reminds me of the beginning of summertime, right when the weather gets warm enough to start craving cold desserts. This is a great recipe to make the night before as it needs to firm up for quite some time, plus it is excellent served very cold.

½ recipe <u>Flakey Classic Piecrust</u>

FILLING

4 cups strawberries, sliced

1 cup granulated sugar

4 tablespoons cornstarch

¼ cup water Pinch salt

2 or 3 sliced strawberries for a garnish

- Preheat oven to 425°F. Lightly grease a standard-size pie pan and dust with brown rice or sorghum flour.

- Prepare the pie crust according to recipe directions.

- Roll out the dough in between two pieces of parchment paper until it is about ¼ inch thick. Carefully invert onto a pie pan, shaping to fit and make a lip on the crust. Using a fork, poke about twenty small holes evenly over the crust. Bake for 20 minutes, or until crust is firm. Let cool completely before

filling.

- Filling: Place 1½ cups of the strawberries plus the sugar into a 2-quart saucepan and mash gently with a potato masher. Cook over medium heat just until sugar dissolves completely.

- In a medium bowl, whisk together the cornstarch and water until smooth and add to the cooked strawberry mixture along with the salt. Bring to a boil over medium heat and allow to cook for about 2 minutes. Remove from heat and let cool slightly, but not completely, for about 15 minutes. Arrange the remaining 2½ cups strawberries evenly into the piecrust. Pour the cooked filling into prepared pie pan and let chill in fridge until firm, for about 12 hours. Garnish with additional strawberry slices. Serve cold. Store in airtight container in refrigerator for up to 2 days.

CHERRY PIE

YIELD: 10 SERVINGS

I recommend using Bing or sour cherries for this pie to achieve that lovely deep red color that we're so accustomed to with cherry pie. I particularly love this pie served warm from the oven à la mode.

1 recipe <u>Flakey Classic Piecrust</u>

4 cups fresh cherries, pitted

¼ cup tapioca flour 1 cup sugar

¼ teaspoon salt

1 teaspoon vanilla extract

4 teaspoons non dairy margarine

- Prepare the pie crust according to recipe directions and divide crust evenly into two sections. Refrigerate one disk while you roll out the other in between two sheets of parchment paper, to about ¼ inch thickness. Flip over into a deep-dish pie pan and shape to fit the pan.

- In a large bowl, toss the cherries with the tapioca flour, sugar, salt, and vanilla extract until evenly coated. Place into the pie shell and spread evenly. Dot with margarine. Roll out the other half of the crust in between two sheets of parchment paper to ¼ inch thickness. Drape over the top of the pie, inverting using one sheet of parchment to assist, and top the pie with the second crust. Flute the edges to seal and then slice a few small slits in the crust to vent. Bake for 45 to 50 minutes, until pie crust is golden brown. Let pie cool slightly before serving. Store in airtight container for up to 2 days.

You can use frozen cherries if fresh aren't in season; simply thaw them out and drain thoroughly before using.

ANY BERRY PIE

YIELD: 10 SERVINGS

Blackberry, blueberry, raspberry … any type of berry can be used in this pie and it will still be delicious. My favorite is a solid tie between blackberry and blueberry.

1 recipe <u>Flakey Classic Piecrust</u>

½ cup brown sugar

¼ cup sugar

3 tablespoons cornstarch

½ teaspoon salt

1 teaspoon vanilla extract

4 cups blackberries, blueberries, or raspberries

1 tablespoon non dairy margarine

- Preheat oven to 425°F.

- Prepare the crust according to recipe directions and roll out half of the crust in between two sheets of parchment to ¼ inch thick, while keeping the other half chilled. Place one half of crust into a deep-dish pie pan and shape to fit the pie pan.

- In a medium bowl, toss together the brown sugar, sugar, cornstarch, and salt until well mixed. Add in the vanilla extract and berries and gently stir until the berries are completed covered. Place berries into the piecrust and dot evenly with margarine.

- Roll out the other half of pie crust in between two sheets of parchment until about ¼ inch thick. Work fast! Have a pizza cutter handy and slice 1 × 9-inch strips of pie crust. Use your hands to gently peel up the tip of the strip and drape on top of the blueberries to form a crosshatch pattern until pie is covered to your liking. You can also use a cookie cutter to cut out shapes to top the pie.

- Bake for 40 minutes, or until the piecrust is deep golden brown, but not burned. Serve hot à la mode or room temperature. Store in airtight container for up to 2 days.

TARTE TATIN

YIELD: 8 SERVINGS

This recipe is super simple but requires a pan that can safely, and effectively, go from stove top to oven, such as cast iron. For a perfect Tarte Tatin, choose a variety of apple that will hold its shape while cooking, such as Granny Smith or Gala.

½ recipe <u>Flakey Classic Piecrust</u>

¼ cup non dairy margarine

½ cup brown sugar

5 small apples, peeled, cored, and quartered

* Preheat oven to 425°F. Shape the pie crust dough into a disk and chill until ready to use.

* Over medium heat, in a 9-inch cast-iron pan, melt the margarine until liquid. Sprinkle on the brown sugar and then place the apples directly on top of the sugar, arranging snugly and evenly so that the domed sides are facing down. Try to eliminate any excess spaces in between the apples. Let the apples cook, completely undisturbed over medium heat for 20 minutes.

* Transfer the hot pan to the oven and bake on the middle rack for 20 more minutes.

- Remove from oven and let rest briefly.

- Roll the pie crust out in between two sheets of parchment paper, just wide enough to cover the cast-iron pan with about 1 inch excess. Flip the piecrust over the apples to cover, and push the dough gently down to form a rustic top crust. Bake for an additional 20 minutes, and then remove from oven and let cool for 10 minutes.

- Flip the pie out onto a lipped plate, roughly the same size as the tart. The dough will invert to form a lovely crust. If any apples happen to stick to the pan, carefully remove and place them back onto the tart.

- Serve warm or room temperature. Store in airtight container for up to 2 days.

CHOCOLATE SILK PIE

YIELD: 10 SERVINGS

This is one of my favorite desserts to bring to potlucks because of its simplicity and versatility. The secret ingredient is silken tofu, which creates a base that's both firm and silky. Top each individual piece with Sweetened Whipped Coconut Cream just before serving.

½ recipe <u>Flakey Classic Piecrust</u>

2 (350 g) packages extra-firm silken tofu

2 teaspoons vanilla extract

2 tablespoons cocoa powder (I like extra-dark)

½ cup sugar

1½ cups chopped non dairy chocolate or chocolate chips

- Preheat oven to 400°F.

- Prepare the pie crust according to recipe directions and roll out in between two sheets of parchment paper until about ¼ inch thick.

- Flip over the parchment to gently place the crust into a standard-size glass pie pan. Fold or flute the crust and pierce bottom several times evenly with fork. Bake for 20 minutes, or until light golden brown. Remove from oven.

- To prepare the filling, blend the tofu, vanilla extract, cocoa powder, and sugar in a food processor until completely smooth, scraping down sides as needed.

- In a double boiler, melt the chocolate and drizzle into the tofu mixture and blend until completely incorporated. Spread filling into baked pie shell and let cool at room temperature for 1 hour before transferring to the refrigerator to chill until slightly firm, 4 hours up to overnight. Store in airtight container in refrigerator for up to 3 days.

SKY-HIGH PEANUT BUTTER PIE

YIELD: 10 SERVINGS

If you love peanut butter you're going to flip over this pie. Rich peanut butter and chocolate combine for a luscious base, while fluffy coconut cream gives the pie its name. You can also switch this up and use almond or cashew butter if you have a peanut allergy.

½ recipe <u>Flakey Classic Piecrust</u>

4 ounces semi-sweet chocolate

3 (350 g) packages firm silken tofu

2 cups creamy peanut butter

2 cups confectioners sugar

3 tablespoons ground chia seed

½ teaspoon sea salt

1 recipe <u>Sweetened Whipped Coconut Cream</u>

2 ounces non dairy chocolate chips or chunks, melted, for drizzling

¼ cup crushed roasted and salted peanuts

- Preheat oven to 400°F and prepare the pie crust according to recipe directions. Roll out in between two sheets of parchment until ¼ inch thick. Drape over a deep-dish pie pan and press down evenly to cover. Flute edges and bake for 20 minutes, or until lightly golden brown. Remove from oven and place on wire rack to cool. Sprinkle 4 ounces of the chocolate chips evenly onto the piecrust and let rest for 5 minutes. Spread the melted chocolate, using a silicone spatula, to coat the inside of the pie crust. Let cool completely until chocolate is rehardened—once the crust is at room temperature, place in the refrigerator to speed up the process.

- In a food processor combine the tofu, peanut butter, sugar, chia seed, and salt. Blend until completely smooth, for about 5 minutes. Spread into the prepared pie crust, and freeze for at least 3 hours. Transfer to refrigerator and chill overnight. Before serving, top with whipped coconut cream and drizzle with chocolate. Sprinkle with crushed peanuts. Store in an airtight container in the refrigerator for up to 2 days.

PECAN PIE

YIELD: 10 SERVINGS

The first time I tasted Pecan Pie, I was smitten. Even today when I get around one, it takes a bit of restraint for me to stop eating the whole darn thing! Best to share with others, or just make two pies, and save yourself the heartache.

½ recipe <u>Flakey Classic Piecrust</u>

2 tablespoons flaxseed meal

¼ cup water

1¼ cups packed brown sugar

2 tablespoons superfine brown rice flour, or white rice flour

2 teaspoons vanilla extract

½ cup melted non dairy margarine

1½ cups chopped pecans

- Preheat oven to 400°F. Prepare the pie crust according to recipe directions and press into a standard-size pie pan, making the crust slightly shorter than the top edge of the pan. Flute or use a spoon to make a design in the top of the crust.

- In a large bowl, stir together flaxseed meal and water and let set for 5 minutes, until gelled. Transfer to a mixing bowl and whip on high speed using a whisk attachment for 1 minute (or using elbow grease and a whisk), until fluffy. Add the sugar, brown rice flour, vanilla extract, and margarine. Fold in 1 cup of the chopped pecans. Stir well. Spoon filling into unbaked crust and then top with remaining chopped pecans.

- Bake for 35 to 40 minutes, until crust is golden brown and filling is bubbly. Carefully remove from the oven and let cool completely, for at least 4 hours, before serving. Store in airtight container in refrigerator for up to 2 days.

CHEESECAKES

NEW YORK–STYLE CHEESECAKE

YIELD: 12 SERVINGS

This cheesecake takes a little added patience as it absolutely must be left in the oven 1 to 2 hours to finish baking and then it must be chilled overnight, but it is so worth it. This classic dessert is just perfect plain but pairs exceptionally well with fruit topping. Try it with Cherry Vanilla Compote, Broiled Persimmons, Blueberry Lavender Jam, or even plain fruit such as strawberries.

¼ cup almond meal

4 (8-ounce) tubs nondairy cream cheese, such as Tofutti brand

1¾ cups sugar

½ cup non dairy sour cream or coconut cream

½ cup besan/chickpea flour mixed with ½ cup water

¼ cup superfine brown rice flour or white rice flour

1 teaspoon vanilla extract

- Preheat oven to 350°F and lightly grease an 8-inch springform pan. Sprinkle the bottom of the pan evenly with the almond meal. You may use a larger pan, but your cheesecake will be thinner and may need to cook less time.

- Place all the remaining ingredients into a food processor and blend until very smooth, for about 2 minutes, scraping down the sides as needed. Don't taste the batter as the besan will make it unpleasant until baked!

- Bake for 45 minutes at 350°F and then reduce heat to 325°F. Bake for an additional 35 minutes, and then turn off oven. Let the cheesecake cool, inside the closed oven, for about 1 to 2 hours. Chill overnight before serving. Store in airtight container in refrigerator for up to 4 days.

PISTACHIO ROSE CHEESECAKE

YIELD: 10 SERVINGS

This fragrant cake is delightful when served with a dollop of Sweetened Whipped Coconut Cream and a dry white wine, or sparkling grape juice for the kids. Rose water can be located in most specialty grocers near other similar extracts and flavorings. Certainly, if you cannot locate this particular flavoring, equal amounts of spiced rum or vanilla extract would replace it just fine, albeit without the floral undertones.

CRUST

1 tablespoon flaxseed meal

2 tablespoons water

1 cup pistachios, pulsed until crumbly

2 tablespoons sugar

1 tablespoon almond or canola oil

¼ cup almond meal, plus extra for sprinkling

FILLING

2 cups (20 ounces) silken tofu

1 to 1½ teaspoons rose water (the more the rosier!)

3 (8-ounce) containers nondairy cream cheese, such as Tofutti

¾ cup sugar

¼ teaspoon salt

3 tablespoons white rice flour

2 drops pink food coloring (optional)

- Preheat oven to 400°F. Lightly grease only the sides of an 8-inch springform pan. You may use a larger pan, but your cheesecake will be thinner and may need to cook less time.

- In a small bowl, combine flaxseed meal with water and let rest until gelled, for about 5 minutes. In a large bowl, mix together the pistachios, sugar, almond oil, almond meal, and prepared flaxseed meal until clumpy. Use very lightly greased hands and press firmly into the bottom of the springform pan and cover as best as you can. Once it is spread out covering as much surface as possible, sprinkle lightly with almond meal and then press down to cover completely and evenly.

- In a food processor, combine all the ingredients for the filling and blend until completely smooth, for about 5 minutes, scraping down sides often. Spread the filling evenly into the prepared springform pan and then bake for 15 minutes.

- Reduce heat to 250°F, without removing the cheesecake from the oven, and bake for an additional 60 minutes. Turn oven off and let cheesecake remain for 1 more hour. Let cool for 1 hour at room temperature on a wire rack and then transfer to the refrigerator to cool overnight. Store in airtight container in refrigerator for up to 4 days.

CARAMEL CHAI CHEESECAKE

YIELD: 10 SERVINGS

This version of the classic dessert is pure decadence. If you really love cinnamon, cloves, and allspice, serve it with a piping-hot mug of chai for the ultimate spicy indulgence.

CRUST

6 ounces (170 g) pecans

3 tablespoons melted non dairy margarine

3 tablespoons sugar

2 tablespoons superfine brown rice flour

FILLING

1 (350 g) package extra-firm silken tofu

3 (8-ounce) tubs nondairy cream cheese, such as Tofutti

⅔ cup packed light brown sugar

5 tablespoons superfine brown rice flour

¼ teaspoon sea salt

1 teaspoon cinnamon

⅛ teaspoon allspice

¼ teaspoon ground black pepper

¼ teaspoon ground cloves

⅛ teaspoon cardamom

1 teaspoon vanilla extract

1 recipe Caramel Sauce

For the Crust

* Preheat oven to 400°F. Pulse the pecans in a food processor, just until crumbly. Stir in the rest of the crust ingredients and press (using hands dusted with superfine brown rice flour) into an 8-inch springform pan.

* Bake for 10 minutes and then remove from the oven.

For the Filling

* Place all the ingredients for the filling into a food processor and blend until very smooth, for at least 5 minutes. Spread onto the prepared crust and bake in preheated oven for 15 minutes. Reduce heat to 250°F and allow cheesecake to bake for an additional 60 minutes. Turn oven off and let cool for up to 2 more hours while remaining in the oven. Chill in refrigerator overnight and

then make the Caramel Sauce just before serving, so that you have hot caramel sauce on a cold cheesecake. Top with Sweetened Whipped Coconut Cream. Store in airtight container in refrigerator for up to 4 days.

PUMPKIN PECAN CHEESECAKE

YIELD: 12 SERVINGS

What could be more apropos for autumn than this flavor combo? If you're looking for a wonderful alternative (or addition!) to Pumpkin Pie on Thanksgiving, look no further.

CRUST

1 tablespoon flaxseed meal

2 tablespoons water

2 cups pecans

¼ teaspoon salt

¼ cup brown sugar

FILLING

1 block firm silken tofu

2 (8-ounce) tubs nondairy cream cheese, such as Tofutti

1 cup sugar

¼ cup plus 2 tablespoons brown rice flour

¼ cup lemon juice

1 (15-ounce) can pumpkin puree

⅓ cup brown sugar

1 teaspoon cinnamon

½ teaspoon pumpkin pie spice

- Preheat oven to 400°F. Lightly grease the sides of an 8-inch springform pan.

- In a small bowl, mix together the flaxseed meal and the water. Let rest for 5 minutes, until gelled. In a food processor, pulse together the pecans, salt, and brown sugar until the mixture resembles coarse crumbles. Add in prepared flaxseed meal and pulse again until pecans come together into a loose dough. Press into the bottom of the prepared springform pan and bake for 10 minutes.

- In the meantime, clean the food processor and mix together the tofu, non dairy cream cheese, sugar, ¼ cup brown rice flour, and lemon juice. Blend until completely smooth, for about 2 minutes, scraping down sides as needed. Scoop out about 1 cup of this mixture and spread evenly onto the crust to form a thin white layer. Add the canned pumpkin, brown sugar, cinnamon, pumpkin pie spice, and remaining 2 tablespoons brown rice flour. Blend again until completely smooth, scraping down sides as needed. Spread on top of white layer.

- Bake for 15 minutes. Reduce oven temperature to 325°F and bake for an additional hour. Turn oven off and let cheesecake remain for about 1 hour. Chill completely overnight before serving. Store in airtight container in refrigerator for up to 3 days.

CHOCOLATE BROWNIE CHEESECAKE

YIELD: 10 SERVINGS

This cheesecake has a super-secret special ingredient: black beans! But you can't tell—in gluten-free baking, oftentimes beans and legumes can be our best friends, providing a little bit of rise and a lot of binding power, along with a totally neutral flavor, so you won't taste anything but chocolaty goodness.

CRUST

1 cup hazelnut meal (finely ground hazelnuts)

2 tablespoons cocoa powder

3 tablespoons sugar

3 tablespoons melted non dairy margarine or coconut oil

FILLING

⅔ cup sugar

3 (8-ounce) tubs nondairy cream cheese, such as Tofutti

1 cup canned black beans, drained and rinsed

½ cup non dairy milk

¼ cup brown rice flour

2 cups non dairy chocolate chips, melted

- Grease the sides of an 8-inch springform pan and preheat oven to 400°F.

- In a small bowl, stir together the hazelnut meal, cocoa powder, and sugar. Drizzle in the melted margarine and stir to combine. Press the mixture onto the bottom of the springform pan to form an even layer. Bake for 9 minutes.

Remove from oven and decrease temperature to 375°F.

- In a food processor, combine all the ingredients for the filling, one at a time, in the order listed, making sure that all the ingredients have been completely blended before adding in the melted chocolate chips.

- Spread filling mixture evenly on top of the prebaked crust. Bake for 30 minutes, and then reduce oven temperature to 325°F. Bake for an additional 40 minutes. Turn oven off and allow cheesecake to remain for 2 hours. Chill completely—overnight is best—before serving. Store in airtight container in refrigerator for up to 4 days.

TARTS, COBBLERS, AND PASTRIES

CHOCOLATE PISTACHIO TART

YIELD: 8 SERVINGS

I love the contrast of the deep chocolate filling against the salty pistachio crust. This pie freezes beautifully and can be thawed in the refrigerator overnight the day before serving.

CRUST

2 tablespoons flaxseed meal 3 tablespoons water

1 cup pistachios, pulsed until crumbly (plus additional crushed pistachios for garnish)

3 tablespoons fine yellow cornmeal

2 scant tablespoons sugar

½ teaspoon salt

3 tablespoons olive oil

FILLING

2½ cups nondairy semi-sweet chocolate chips

1⅓ cups coconut milk

1 teaspoon vanilla extract

⅛ teaspoon ground cumin

¼ teaspoon sea salt

- Preheat oven to 400°F.

- In a small bowl, combine the flaxseed meal with the water and let rest until gelled, for about 5 minutes. In a separate small bowl, whisk together the pistachios, cornmeal, sugar, and salt until well combined. Evenly mix in the olive oil and flaxseed gel, using clean hands.

- Press crust into a standard-size pie pan, about ⅛ inch thick. Bake for 10 minutes. Remove and let cool completely.

- To make the filling, place the chocolate chips in a large heat-safe bowl.

- In a small saucepan, combine the coconut milk, vanilla extract, cumin, and salt and bring just to a boil over medium heat. Once bubbly, pour over chocolate chips and mix well. Spread the chocolate mixture into the piecrust and let cool at room temperature, for about 1 hour. Sprinkle with crushed pistachios and transfer into the refrigerator to cool completely until firm. Store in airtight container in refrigerator for up to 2 days.

PEARBERRY TART

YIELD: 8 SERVINGS

This fruity concoction is pretty and delish! I recommend red raspberries as they look so beautiful against the amber-colored pears. The tart is easy to prep, and it has a silky custard texture that will make you yearn for a second slice!

½ recipe <u>Flakey Classic Piecrust</u>

⅓ cup besan/chickpea flour

3 tablespoons cornstarch

⅓ cup sugar

½ teaspoon salt

1 cup red raspberries or other berry

2 medium pears, peeled, cored, and sliced

⅓ cup turbinado sugar

- Preheat oven to 400°F.

- Prepare the piecrust as directed and chill in refrigerator for 30 minutes. Roll out in between two sheets of parchment paper to about ¼ inch thick. Flip over onto an 8-inch tart shell and press dough into the pan, trimming any excess.

- In a medium bowl, whisk together the besan, cornstarch, sugar, and salt. Rinse

79

the berries and dredge them in the flour mixture to evenly coat. Remove and set aside. Toss the sliced pears into the mixture as well and then rustically (no fancy pattern needed) arrange the pears and berries into the tart shell. Top with an even layer of turbinado sugar. Bake for 35 to 40 minutes, or until crust is golden brown on edges. Store in airtight container in refrigerator for up to 2 days.

ALMOND APPLE TART

YIELD: 4 SERVINGS

This elegant dessert, which features the fragrant combination of almonds and apples, comes together effortlessly if you already have some puff pastry frozen. You'll have a fancy dessert ready to impress in no time flat. This tart also keeps well if refrigerated for up to 1 week; simply reheat at 350°F for 10 minutes and sprinkle with a touch of turbinado sugar before serving.

½ recipe Puff Pastry

2 tablespoons turbinado sugar

1 large Granny Smith apple, peeled and thinly sliced

1 teaspoon lemon or lime juice

½ cup brown sugar, plus 2 tablespoons for sprinkling on top

1 teaspoon vanilla extract

⅛ teaspoon salt

3 tablespoons cornstarch

2 tablespoons almond meal

- Place a rectangle of chilled puff pastry dough in between two sheets of parchment paper and gently roll out into a rectangle about 5 × 8 inches. Transfer the dough to a baking sheet lined with parchment paper or a silicone mat. Crimp up the edges of the crust to form a lip, gently folding the top back onto itself. Sprinkle evenly with the 2 tablespoons turbinado sugar.

- In a medium bowl, toss the apples with the lemon juice, and then with the remaining ingredients, until the apples are well coated. Arrange the apples onto the tart shell in an even layer, overlapping each slice to form a pattern. Sprinkle with the 2 tablespoons brown sugar.

- Bake for 35 to 40 minutes, or until apples are tender and crust is golden brown. Store in airtight container for up to 2 days.

CRANBERRY WHITE CHOCOLATE CITRUS TART

YIELD: 10 SERVINGS

White chocolate and cranberry is a popular combination; the addition of orange here creates a nice tang. You can make your own dairy-free white chocolate for this tart or seek out your favorite brand elsewhere.

CRUST

1¾ cups almond meal

¼ cup brown sugar

3 tablespoons coconut oil, liquid

Dash salt

TOPPING

1½ cups fresh cranberries

¼ cup sugar

FILLING

2 cups raw cashews, soaked at least 3 hours and drained

¼ cup sugar

½ cup orange juice

1 teaspoon orange zest

5.5 ounces (150 g) non dairy white chocolate

For the Crust

- Preheat oven to 400°F.

- In a small bowl, mix together the almond meal and brown sugar. Stir in the melted coconut oil and salt until completely mixed. Use lightly greased hands or the bottom of a drinking glass and press the mixture into an 8-inch tart pan.

- Bake the crust for 10 minutes in your preheated oven. Remove from the oven and let cool completely.

For the Topping

- Combine the cranberries and sugar in a small saucepan and cook over medium heat, stirring often, until sugar granules have dissolved completely. Increase temperature slightly to reduce until thickened, for about 5 minutes.

For the Filling

- In a food processor, blend the cashews with the sugar, orange juice, and zest until very, very smooth, for about 5 minutes. Over a double boiler, melt the white chocolate and then blend with the rest of the ingredients.

- Quickly spread the cashew filling into the cooled tart crust and top with the cranberry mixture. Gently run a knife through the top of the filling to swirl through. Chill in the refrigerator until firm. Store in airtight container in refrigerator for up to 2 days.

WHITE CHOCOLATE PEANUT BUTTER PRETZEL TARTLETS

YIELD: 12 TARTS

Salty pretzels pair so wonderfully with the combined sweetness of white chocolate and peanut butter and are presented in a cute little tartlet package.

1½ cups crushed gluten-free pretzels

6 tablespoons softened non dairy margarine

2 tablespoons sugar

1 cup non dairy white chocolate chips

½ cup smooth peanut butter

¼ cup canned coconut milk

1 cup non dairy milk

* Preheat oven to 350°F. Gather about twelve 2-inch tart pans and lightly spray with nonstick cooking oil.

* Combine the crushed pretzels, margarine, and sugar together until very well mixed. Make sure there are no lumps of margarine. When pressed, the mixture should hold its shape. You may need to add a touch more margarine if it feels too crumbly ... but just about a tablespoon or so.

- Gently press the crumbs into the tart pans, making an even crust that is about ¼ inch thick. Handle with care.

- Bake for about 12 minutes, or until dark golden brown. Remove tart shells from oven and let cool on wire racks.

- Once the crusts are cool, begin making your filling.

- Place white chocolate chips into a medium bowl. In a small saucepan, combine the peanut butter, coconut milk, and nondairy milk and cook over medium heat, stirring constantly using a wire whisk.

- Once the mixture just begins to bubble and is very hot, pour over white chocolate chips, stirring quickly to melt. Spoon into the prepared tart shells, allowing to cool at room temperature for about an hour before transferring to the refrigerator to chill completely. Store in airtight container in refrigerator for up to 2 days.

PEACHY KEEN COBBLER

YIELD: 8 SERVINGS

This cobbler is a perfect way to use up a bunch of fruit, especially when you have a lotta hard peaches rolling around—which tends to happen to me quite often during the summertime (I over purchase and don't want to wait for all of them to ripen!). Any stone fruit can be used; try this recipe with plums or apricots, too!

4 peaches (about 4½ cups) peeled and sliced

½ cup sugar

¼ teaspoon ground allspice

3 tablespoons cornstarch

⅓ cup potato starch

⅓ cup white rice flour

⅓ cup besan/chickpea flour

1 teaspoon xanthan gum

1 teaspoon baking powder

3 tablespoons sugar

6 tablespoons non dairy margarine

¼ cup + 2 tablespoons non dairy milk

1 teaspoon lemon juice

- Preheat oven to 375°F and lightly grease a small stoneware or ceramic baking dish, about 5 × 9 inches.

- In a medium bowl, toss together the peaches, sugar, allspice, and cornstarch. Arrange in the greased baking dish in an even layer.

- In a separate bowl, whisk together the potato starch, white rice flour, besan, xanthan gum, baking powder, and sugar. Cut in the margarine and blend using a pastry blender until even crumbles form. Add in the nondairy milk and lemon juice and stir until smooth.

- Drop by heaping spoonfuls on top of the sliced peaches. Bake for 35 to 40 minutes, or until bubbly and the biscuit top is golden brown on edges. Store in airtight container for up to 1 day.

CHERRY CLAFOUTIS

YIELD: 8 SERVINGS

This recipe is such a perfect use for fresh cherries as this dessert truly accentuates the color and flavor of the short-seasoned fresh fruit. Cherries not in season? Good news: frozen cherries work, too! Thanks to Lydia, who tested for this cookbook, for the tip.

½ block extra-firm tofu, drained but not pressed (about 215 g)

1½ cups besan/chickpea flour

1½ cups non dairy milk

1 teaspoon baking powder

2 tablespoons tapioca flour

¾ cup sugar

¾ teaspoon sea salt

1 teaspoon vanilla extract

2 cups pitted cherries

¼ cup confectioners sugar

- Preheat oven to 350°F and grease an 8-inch cast-iron skillet or glass pie pan with enough margarine to coat.

- Place all the ingredients but the cherries and the confectioner's sugar into a blender and blend until the mixture is uniform and very smooth, scraping down sides as needed. Pour the batter into the prepared pan and then dot evenly with pitted cherries, placing them about ½ inch apart on top of the batter.

- Bake for 50 to 55 minutes, or until a knife inserted into the middle comes out clean. Let cool completely and dust with confectioners sugar before serving. Store in airtight container for up to 2 days in refrigerator.

APPLE CRISP

YIELD: 6 SERVINGS

This simple and rustic dessert is as easy to whip up as it is delicious. Serve à la mode for an over-the-top treat. My favorite type of apple to use in this is Granny Smith, but any crisp variety will do.

5 apples, peeled and sliced ½ to ¼ inch thick

¾ cup brown sugar

½ cup brown rice flour

¼ cup potato starch

1 teaspoon cinnamon

¾ cup certified gluten-free oats

⅓ cup non dairy margarine

- Preheat oven to 375°F. Lightly grease a ceramic baking dish or cake pan, about 8 × 8 inches. Arrange the sliced apples evenly to cover the bottom of the baking dish.

- In a medium bowl, whisk together the brown sugar, brown rice flour, potato starch, cinnamon, and oats. Cut in the margarine using a pastry blender until crumbly. Sprinkle liberally over the apples.

- Bake for 35 to 40 minutes, until golden brown and bubbly. Store in airtight container in refrigerator for up to 2 days.

MILLE-FEUILLE

YIELD: 8 SERVINGS

Elegant and classy, this French dessert will make your dinner guests do a double take. Even though it looks complicated, it's really quite easy once you have the puff pastry prepared. Just assemble and serve!

½ recipe <u>Puff Pastry</u>

½ recipe <u>Mascarpone</u>

1 cup confectioners sugar

½ cup <u>Strawberry Preserves</u>

¼ cup cacao nibs

½ cup melted chocolate

Strawberries for garnish

- Preheat oven to 400°F. Line a large baking sheet with parchment or a silicone mat. Roll out the puff pastry into a rectangle about ¼ inch thick. Chill briefly in the freezer, for about 10 minutes, and then carefully cut into even-size rectangles, about 2.5 × 4 inches. Using a flat metal spatula, carefully transfer the puff pastry to the prepared baking sheet, about ½ inch apart. Bake for 15 to 20 minutes, until puffed and golden brown. Let cool completely and then assemble the dessert.

- Mix the Mascarpone with the confectioner's sugar and place into a pastry bag equipped with a star tip. Glaze the tops of each pastry rectangles with Strawberry Preserves and then pipe on circles of the Mascarpone mixture until the top of the rectangle is covered. Sprinkle with cacao nibs. Top with another strawberry preserve–glazed pastry rectangle and again, pipe another layer of mascarpone and sprinkle with cacao nibs. Top with a final rectangle of pastry glazed with strawberry preserves and then drizzle with melted chocolate. Top with a halved strawberry. Chill for 1 hour in refrigerator and then serve cold.

MINI MAPLE DONUTS

YIELD: 24 DONUTS

If anything can take me back to the donut shop as a kid, it's these guys. These basic cake donuts have a hint of maple—not too cloying. The glaze also goes well with a variety of other desserts, such as the Devil's Food Cake, Maple Cookies, or even the Classic Chocolate Chip Cookies.

DONUTS

⅓ cup + 2 tablespoons sorghum flour

⅓ cup + 2 tablespoons potato starch

¼ cup tapioca flour

¼ cup brown rice flour

¾ teaspoon xanthan gum

½ teaspoon salt

1 teaspoon baking powder

3 tablespoons olive oil

⅓ cup + 1 tablespoon maple syrup

½ cup brown sugar

⅓ cup + 2 tablespoons non dairy milk

1 tablespoon apple cider vinegar

GLAZE

1¼ cups confectioner's sugar

2 tablespoons non dairy milk

1 teaspoon light corn syrup

1 teaspoon maple syrup

1 teaspoon maple extract

Dash salt

- Preheat oven to 325°F and place your oven rack in the middle of the oven. Lightly grease a mini-size donut pan.

- Combine all the ingredients through the salt into a medium mixing bowl and whisk until well combined. Gradually add in the rest of the donut ingredients, in the order given, and mix well until no lumps remain. You should end up with a tacky batter. Fill the cups of the donut pan with batter. Bake for 25 minutes. Let cool completely and then glaze.

- To make the glaze, simply whisk together all ingredients until smooth. Cover cooled donuts completely with glaze and then place onto a wire rack to firm up. Let glaze harden completely before serving. Store in airtight container for up to 4 days.

I like to use corn syrup in my glazes as it truly re-creates that donut-shop texture; however, you may replace the corn syrup with 1 teaspoon maple syrup, which will cause the glaze texture to have a slight variation.

BELGIAN WAFFLES

YIELD: 7 WAFFLES

Of course, you don't need a Belgian waffle maker to enjoy these, any type will do, but they are definitely better bigger! Top with your favorite toppings... I'm partial to Cherry Vanilla Compote or Sweetened Whipped Coconut Cream.

1 cup sorghum flour

½ cup superfine brown rice flour

¼ cup potato starch

¼ cup tapioca flour

1 teaspoon xanthan gum

4 tablespoons sugar

4 teaspoons baking powder

¾ teaspoon salt

2 tablespoons lemon juice

5 tablespoons olive oil

1 teaspoon vanilla extract

½ cup canned full-fat coconut milk

1½ cups water

- In a medium bowl, whisk together the sorghum flour, superfine brown rice flour, potato starch, tapioca flour, xanthan gum, sugar, baking powder, and salt.

- Form a well in the center of the flour mixture and add the lemon juice, olive oil, vanilla extract, coconut milk, and water.

- Stir gently with a fork until all ingredients are combined, and then use a whisk to make the batter completely smooth.

- Heat your Belgian waffle maker and lightly mist with nonstick cooking spray. Pour about 1¼ cups batter (depending on your waffle maker's size) and close. Cook for about 2 minutes, or until waffle is golden brown and easily releases from the waffle iron.

APPLE FRITTERS

YIELD: 15 FRITTERS

Like pocket-size apple pies, these crunchy fritters are hard to resist! I love making these when I over purchase during apple season as this is a great recipe to get friends and family to gobble up all those extra apples quickly! You'll need a deep fryer for these to achieve a perfect crunch and quick, even cooking throughout.

3 apples, peeled

1 cup besan/chickpea flour, plus ½ cup for dredging

⅔ cup sugar

⅔ cup non dairy milk

½ teaspoon salt

½ teaspoon cinnamon Oil for frying

Turbinado and confectioner's sugar for dusting

- Preheat deep fryer to 360°F. Slice apples into ¼- to ½-inch-thick circles and use a small circular cookie cutter or apple corer to remove the seeds to form rings.

- In a medium-size bowl, whisk together the besan, sugar, non dairy milk, salt, and cinnamon until smooth. Once the fryer is ready, dredge the apple slices in the extra besan and then dip into the batter to completely coat.

- Fry apples three to four at a time for 5 minutes, flipping over two-thirds of the way through cooking time. Transfer to a paper towel– or paper bag– lined baking sheet (they will be soft at first) and then sprinkle with turbinado and confectioner's sugar. Repeat until all batter/apple slices have been fried.

- Let cool for at least 10 minutes before serving. Serve the same day, best within 1 hour of preparing.

STRAWBERRY TOASTER PASTRIES

YIELD: 6 PASTRIES

As a kid, I was obsessed with boxed toaster pastries, but, as I grew older and wiser about food, I became quite unimpressed with their extremely long ingredient lists. These pastries are just as tasty without the unpronounceable ingredients. You'll also find a brown sugar variation below.

FILLING

3 tablespoons strawberry jam

1½ teaspoons cornstarch mixed with

1½ teaspoons water

Dash salt

1 recipe Flakey Classic Piecrust

1 tablespoon flaxseed meal

2½ tablespoons water

- In a small bowl, combine the ingredients for the filling until smooth. Preheat oven to 350°F.

- Prepare the Flakey Classic Pie Crust according to recipe directions and chill for about 15 minutes in the freezer. Roll out in between two sheets of parchment paper until the dough is about ¼ inch thick. Use a pizza wheel or large flat knife to cut the dough into twelve even rectangles, about 3 × 4 inches wide; use a metal spatula to help transfer six of the rectangles to a parchment or silicone mat covered cookie sheet. Place the rectangles about 1 inch apart.

- Combine the flaxseed meal and water and let rest until thickened, for about 5 minutes. Lightly brush the tops of the rectangles on the cookie sheet with the flaxseed gel. Place about 1½ tablespoons filling into the center of the six rectangles. Use a spatula to help transfer the remaining six rectangles to cover each mound of filling.

- Crimp the sides of the dough to seal using the tines of a fork. Brush the tops lightly with additional flaxseed gel and poke about seven holes in the tops of each pastry. Bake for 30 to 35 minutes, or until golden brown on edges. Let cool completely and toast in toaster oven before serving. Top with Royal Icing or leave plain. Store in airtight container for up to 2 days.

BROWN SUGAR CINNAMON VARIATION

¼ cup brown sugar

½ teaspoon cinnamon

2 tablespoons brown rice flour

Whisk together the ingredients and use in place of the strawberry filling in the recipe. Top with Vanilla Glaze or Maple Glaze.

FABULOUS FROZEN TREATS

Chill out with the cool treats on the following pages. Whether you're craving a sweet fix during the summertime, or you just need some fuel to help you veg out during a wintertime movie marathon, you'll be glad to have these recipes on hand (or in your freezer) when the craving strikes. You may be surprised that non dairy milks, such as almond, cashew, and coconut, do a remarkable job of replicating that creamy dreamy texture we crave from traditional-style ice cream. When choosing alternative milks for your ice cream, just like traditional ice cream, the higher the fat content the better!

Making Ice Cream Without a Machine

While it is possible to make ice cream without an ice cream machine, I do recommend sourcing an ice cream maker (from hand-crank to fully electric) if you make your own frequently, as I do. It is the best way to create unique flavors that are hard to come by in dairy-/egg-free versions at the supermarket or local gelataria.

I recommend using a machine only because of the amount of air that is able to be incorporated into the mix as it freezes, resulting in a lighter, airier texture, which is difficult to replicate without a machine. It is, however, easy to come pretty close. Most important, I recommend starting with a base that has a heavy fat content, such as the Vanilla Soft Serve or Chocolate Hazelnut Ice Cream. This will help reduce the odds of ice crystals forming while freezing, producing a smoother, creamier treat. Also, dropping a touch of alcohol (such as vodka or bourbon) into the mix, or using a recipe that incorporates alcohol before freezing will also help reduce crystallization.

Follow the directions for preparing your chosen recipe, and then place the mixture into a stainless steel or glass bowl and chill completely in the refrigerator, up to 8 hours. Whisk thoroughly to stir and then pour the mixture into a nonstick pan (plastic works well), stirring with a whisk after adding. Cover lightly with plastic wrap. Let the mixture chill in the freezer for 30 minutes, and then whisk again. You can incorporate more air by using an electric hand mixer for mixing. Chill for another 30 minutes, and then whisk (or blend) again. Repeat until the ice cream is frozen through and creamy. Transfer to a flexible airtight container. Most ice creams will last in the freezer for about 3 months.

ICE CREAM AND GELATO

VANILLA SOFT SERVE

YIELD: 1 PINT

I absolutely adore flavors and add-ins of all kinds but, if I had to pick a favorite ice cream flavor, it wouldn't be anything fancy, just plain ol' vanilla. This ice cream is rich and dreamy and has a light vanilla flavor that lingers.

1 cup sugar

1 tablespoon agave

½ teaspoon xanthan gum

2 tablespoons vanilla extract

2 tablespoons coconut oil or non dairy margarine

1 cup non dairy milk (recommend almond or cashew)

1 cup canned full-fat coconut milk

- In a large bowl, whisk together the sugar, agave, xanthan gum, vanilla extract, coconut oil, and nondairy milk. Transfer to a blender and process until totally smooth. Whisk in the 1 cup coconut milk and process in an ice cream maker according to manufacturer's instructions or process according to the directions in this book. Once blended, store in airtight, flexible container and freeze at least 6 hours before serving. Keeps for up to 3 months frozen.

CHOCOLATE ESPRESSO ICE CREAM

YIELD: 1 QUART

This distinctive dessert is just like an indulgent drink at a coffee shop—so dark and creamy, it will have you requesting a doppio!

⅔ cup non dairy sour cream or plain yogurt

1 cup confectioners sugar

½ cup cocoa powder

2 teaspoons espresso powder

1 (13.5-ounce) can full-fat coconut milk

¼ teaspoon salt

* In a large bowl, whisk together all the ingredients until completely smooth and absolutely no lumps remain. Process in an ice cream maker according to manufacturer's instructions, or process according to the directions <u>in this book</u>. Transfer to a flexible airtight container and freeze at least 6 hours before serving. Keeps for up to 3 months frozen.

BUTTER PECAN ICE CREAM

YIELD: 1 QUART

When I think of Butter Pecan Ice Cream, I think of my father. I'm not sure if it was his favorite flavor, but we always seemed to have a carton of it in the freezer when I was growing up, which undoubtedly helped make it one of *my* favorite flavors of ice cream.

1 cup pecans

1 cup brown sugar

1 (13.5-ounce) can full-fat coconut milk

1 tablespoon non dairy margarine

¼ teaspoon xanthan gum

½ teaspoon salt

1 teaspoon vanilla extract

2 cups almond milk

1 tablespoon cornstarch

1 tablespoon water

- Preheat oven to 400°F. Spread the pecans evenly onto a metal baking sheet and toast for 7 minutes, or until fragrant. Let cool, chop, and set aside.

- In a 2-quart saucepan, whisk together the brown sugar, coconut milk, margarine, xanthan gum, salt, and vanilla extract. Heat the mixture over medium-high heat until the sugar is dissolved and the margarine is melted. Add the almond milk. In a small bowl, whisk together the cornstarch and water to mix well. Stir the cornstarch slurry into the saucepan and continue to heat over medium heat. Stir constantly until the mixture coats the back of a spoon. Remove from heat and transfer to a metal bowl. Place in refrigerator and chill the mixture until cold.

- Process in an ice cream maker according to manufacturer's instructions, or process according to the directions in this book. Once the ice cream is finished processing in the ice cream maker, fold in the toasted pecans. Transfer to a flexible airtight container and freeze for 6 hours. Store in the freezer for up to 2 months.

CHOCOLATE HAZELNUT ICE CREAM

YIELD: 1 PINT

Use store-bought or homemade chocolate hazelnut butter for this recipe.

½ cup non dairy chocolate hazelnut butter, such as Justin's brand

1 cup non dairy milk

2 tablespoons coconut oil

½ teaspoon xanthan gum

⅛ teaspoon salt

½ cup turbinado sugar

½ cup plain non dairy yogurt

- Place all the ingredients into a blender and blend until smooth, scraping the sides of the blender as needed. Process in your ice cream maker according to manufacturer's instructions or follow the directions <u>in this book</u>. Transfer to an airtight flexible container and store in freezer for at least 6 hours. Keeps for up to 3 months frozen.

BUTTERY BROWN SUGAR ICE CREAM

YIELD: 1 QUART

This ice cream proves you can have all of the indulgence of a buttery sweet flavor—without any of the dairy.

¼ cup non dairy margarine

1 cup brown sugar (light or dark)

½ teaspoon xanthan gum

1¾ cups canned full-fat coconut milk

½ teaspoon vanilla extract

⅔ cup non dairy milk

- Heat the margarine, brown sugar, xanthan gum, coconut milk, and vanilla extract just until sugar is dissolved and margarine is melted over medium heat. Stir in the nondairy milk and blend in blender. Chill for about 15 minutes, and then transfer into an ice cream maker. Following the manufacturer's instructions, process the ice cream until completely frozen, or process according to the directions in this book. Transfer to a flexible airtight container and chill in freezer for at least 6 hours. Store in the freezer for up to 3 months.

STRAWBERRY ICE CREAM

YIELD: 1 QUART

Forget the artificially flavored stuff, the only way to go with strawberry ice cream is with real strawberries! This is as authentic as you can get with the help of silken tofu and coconut milk to give it extra creaminess.

2 cups whole strawberries, stems removed

1 block (12.3 ounces) firm silken tofu

1 (13.5-ounce) can full-fat coconut milk 1 teaspoon vanilla extract

¾ cup sugar

1 teaspoon coconut oil

1 cup strawberries, chopped into ½-inch pieces

- Place the 2 cups strawberries into a blender along with the silken tofu, coconut milk, vanilla extract, sugar, and coconut oil. Blend until smooth and then transfer into the bowl of an ice cream maker and process according to manufacturer's instructions, or follow the method <u>in this book</u>. Once the mixture is mostly frozen, mash the remaining 1 cup strawberries and mix into the ice cream. Continue to process until frozen and then transfer to an airtight flexible container. Freeze 6 hours before serving. Keeps for up to 3 months frozen.

MATCHA CASHEW ICE CREAM

YIELD: 1 QUART

The magical cashew is the stand-in for traditional heavy whipping cream in this creamy confection. Matcha green tea powder adds a distinctive color and flavor, which matches the mellow texture of this ice cream.

2 cups raw cashews

½ cup agave

½ cup non dairy milk

¼ teaspoon salt

1½ teaspoons matcha powder

1 small ripe banana

* Place the cashews in a medium bowl and cover with water. Cap with a dinner plate and let the cashews soak for at least 3 hours, preferably 4.

*

* Drain the cashews and transfer into a food processor along with the remaining ingredients. Blend until very smooth, for about 8 minutes, scraping down the sides often. You can make this even creamier by transferring into a blender and blending until super smooth.

*

- Place in the bowl of an ice cream maker and process according to manufacturer's instructions, or follow directions <u>in this book</u>. Transfer to a flexible airtight container and freeze 6 hours before serving. Keeps for up to 3 months frozen.

MINT CHOCOLATE CHIP ICE CREAM

YIELD: 1 QUART

The brilliant green color of this dessert comes from the addition of fresh spinach, which I swear on my ice cream maker's life you won't taste. Make this even healthier by subbing cacao nibs in place of the mini chocolate chips.

2 cups packed fresh spinach

2 (13.5-ounce) cans full-fat coconut milk

½ cup sugar

½ cup coconut palm sugar

1 tablespoon agave

2 teaspoons peppermint extract

½ cup mini non dairy chocolate chips

Place all ingredients up to the chocolate chips into high-speed blender and blend until very smooth, scraping sides as needed. Pour into the bowl of an ice cream maker and process according to manufacturer's instructions, or follow the directions in this book. Once frozen, fold in the chocolate chips and freeze for at least 6 hours. Store in an airtight flexible container in the freezer for up to 3 months.

BLACK BEAN ICE CREAM

YIELD: 1 QUART

Adzuki beans work well here, too, although they can be harder to source.

1½ cups cooked black beans, rinsed

1 (13.5-ounce) can full-fat coconut milk

¾ cup sugar

1 tablespoon cocoa powder

Pinch of salt

⅛ teaspoon xanthan gum

- In a blender, puree all ingredients until very smooth. Process in your ice cream maker according to manufacturer's instructions, or follow the directions in this book. Store in a flexible airtight container and freeze at least 6 hours before serving. Keeps for up to 3 months frozen.

PUMPKIN PATCH ICE CREAM

YIELD: 1 QUART

The first time I tasted pumpkin flavored ice cream was right after a hayride with my childhood bestie while we were in middle school. It was such a great memory, with the crisp fall chill in the evening breeze and the smell of leaves crunching underneath our feet. Now, each time I taste pumpkin ice cream, I get transported right back to that day, autumnal bliss and all.

1½ cups sugar

1 (13.5-ounce) can full-fat coconut milk

2 teaspoons vanilla extract

1 (15-ounce) can pumpkin puree

1½ teaspoons cinnamon

⅛ teaspoon ground nutmeg

⅛ teaspoon cloves

½ teaspoon salt

- Over medium heat, in a 2-quart saucepan, warm the sugar and coconut milk just until the sugar has completely dissolved. Whisk in the vanilla extract, pumpkin puree, spices, and salt. Process in an ice cream maker according to manufacturer's instructions, or follow the directions in this book. Transfer to a flexible airtight container and freeze at least 6 hours before serving. Store in freezer for up to 3 months.

CHOCOLATE EARL GREY GELATO

YIELD: 1 QUART

This popular flavor combination gets its time to shine in this recipe. The floral notes of Earl Grey are subtle, but unforgettable.

7 Earl Grey tea bags

¾ cup very hot water

1 cup non dairy chocolate chips

¾ cup sugar

1 (13.5-ounce) can full-fat coconut milk

1 tablespoon extra-dark cocoa powder

Dash salt

¼ teaspoon xanthan gum, optional, for creaminess

½ cup non dairy milk

* Steep the tea bags in the hot water for at least 15 minutes. Squeeze and remove the tea bags and set tea aside.

* Place the chocolate chips in a large heat-safe bowl.

* Combine the sugar, coconut milk, cocoa powder, salt, and xanthan gum, if using, in a small saucepan over medium heat. Heat just until hot (do not let boil) and pour over chocolate chips to melt. Add the nondairy milk and prepared tea and stir well to combine. Chill the mixture in the refrigerator for 1 hour.

- Place into an ice cream maker and let run just until thickened to a soft serve ice cream consistency, or follow instructions <u>in this book</u>. Transfer immediately to a flexible airtight container and chill at least 6 hours until firm. Keeps for up to 3 months frozen.

BLACKBERRY CHEESECAKE GELATO

YIELD: 1 QUART

I dare you to take just one bite of this creamy concoction; the flavor is highly addictive. The bright purple hue that comes from the blackberries takes this gelato over the top. If blackberries aren't available, feel free to replace with another type of berry, frozen or fresh—all berries go great with cheesecake-flavored gelato! You can use Sweet Cashew Cream in place of the non dairy cream cheese if you like.

2 cups blackberries

1 cup non dairy cream cheese

1 cup non dairy milk

¾ cup sugar

1½ teaspoons vanilla extract

- Place all ingredients into a blender and blend until smooth. Transfer to the bowl of an ice cream maker and process according to manufacturer's directions, or follow directions <u>in this book</u>. Once frozen, store in a flexible airtight container for up to 2 months.

BUTTERSCOTCH PUDDING POPS

YIELD: 6 POPS

These pudding pops make the perfect warm weather treat with their salty butterscotch base and creamy cool texture. You'll need popsicle molds for these, or you can use silicone ice cube trays for mini-pops, or you can even use small paper cups.

1 recipe <u>Butterscotch Sauce</u>

1 (13.5-ounce) can full-fat coconut milk

2 tablespoons coconut palm sugar

⅛ teaspoon salt

3 tablespoons superfine brown rice flour

- In a 2-quart saucepan over medium heat, combine the Butterscotch Sauce, coconut milk, coconut palm sugar, and salt and whisk well until combined. Heat just until the mixture is hot and all coconut milk and sugar has dissolved. Whisk in the superfine brown rice flour and continue to cook over medium heat, stirring often, until thickened, for 4 to 5 minutes.

- Let cool briefly and then pour into popsicle molds, placing wooden sticks directly into the centers. Freeze overnight before enjoying. Keeps for up to 1 month frozen.

This recipe also makes a delicious Butterscotch Pudding—just don't freeze it! Instead, pour the pudding into serving dishes and refrigerate until set, for about 3 hours.

CLASSIC ICE CREAM SANDWICHES

YIELD: 8 SANDWICHES

This recipe produces a cookie that stands up well to freezing and stays soft once frozen, in a classic ice cream sandwich fashion. The base flavor is chocolate—pair the wafers with your favorite ice cream!

¾ cup cold non dairy margarine

1 cup sugar

1 teaspoon vanilla extract

1 cup sorghum flour

¾ cup cocoa powder

½ cup potato starch

1 teaspoon xanthan gum

¼ teaspoon baking soda

2 tablespoons non dairy milk

4 cups of your favorite non dairy ice cream

* In a large mixing bowl, cream together the margarine, sugar, and vanilla extract. In a separate, smaller mixing bowl mix the sorghum flour, cocoa powder, potato starch, xanthan gum, and baking soda until well combined.

- Gradually incorporate the flour mixture into the sugar mixture until crumbly. Once crumbly, add the non dairy milk until completely combined. If using an electric mixer, just let it ride on low as you add the non dairy milk. Your dough should get quite stiff at this point.

- Shape into a rectangular log, about 2 × 10 inches, using the help of parchment paper and a bench scraper/offset spatula to flatten and form the sides. Wrap loosely with parchment paper and chill in the freezer for 30 minutes, until very cold.

- Preheat oven to 350°F. Once the dough is well chilled, cut the log in half, making two even-sized bricks (about 2 × 5 inches each). Flip each brick on its side, and then slice evenly into rectangles about 2 × 3 inches and about $\frac{1}{8}$ inch thick to emulate a cookie from a store-bought ice cream sandwich.

- As you slice the cookies, place each slab of thin dough gently onto parchment paper or a silpat mat.

- Bake in preheated oven for 14 to 16 minutes. Remove from oven and allow to cool completely at room temperature. Transfer to the freezer just before assembling and chill for at least 10 minutes. Meanwhile, soften your chosen ice cream for about 10 minutes, or until easily scoopable.

- To assemble, take one cookie, and plop a few spoonfuls of your favorite ice cream on top. Smoosh down the ice cream with another cookie and run a spoon around the edge to ensure even distribution of ice cream.

- Return sandwiches to freezer and chill until firm. Once firm, neatly wrap them in waxed paper to store. Keeps for up to 3 months frozen.

METRIC CONVERSIONS

The recipes in this book have not been tested with metric measurements, so some variations might occur.

Remember that the weight of dry ingredients varies according to the volume or density factor: 1 cup of flour weighs far less than 1 cup of sugar, and 1 tablespoon doesn't necessarily hold 3 teaspoons.

General Formula for Metric Conversion

Ounces to grams   multiply ounces by 28.35

Grams to ounces   multiply ounces by 0.035

Pounds to grams   multiply pounds by 453.5

Pounds to kilograms   multiply pounds by 0.45

Cups to liters   multiply cups by 0.24

Fahrenheit to Celsius   subtract 32 from Fahrenheit

temperature, multiply by 5, divide by 9

Celsius to Fahrenheit   multiply Celsius temperature by 9,

divide by 5, add 32

Volume (Liquid) Measurements

1 teaspoon = ⅙ fluid ounce = 5 milliliters

1 tablespoon = ½ fluid ounce = 15 milliliters 2 tablespoons = 1 fluid ounce = 30 milliliters

¼ cup = 2 fluid ounces = 60 milliliters

⅓ cup = 2⅔ fluid ounces = 79 milliliters

½ cup = 4 fluid ounces = 118 milliliters

1 cup or ½ pint = 8 fluid ounces = 250 milliliters

2 cups or 1 pint = 16 fluid ounces = 500 milliliters

4 cups or 1 quart = 32 fluid ounces = 1,000 milliliters

1 gallon = 4 liters

Oven Temperature Equivalents, Fahrenheit (F) and Celsius (C)

100°F = 38°C

200°F = 95°C

250°F = 120°C

300°F = 150°C

350°F = 180°C

400°F = 205°C

450°F = 230°C

Volume (Dry) Measurements

¼ teaspoon = 1 milliliter

½ teaspoon = 2 milliliters

¾ teaspoon = 4 milliliters 1 teaspoon = 5 milliliters

1 tablespoon = 15 milliliters

¼ cup = 59 milliliters

⅓ cup = 79 milliliters

½ cup = 118 milliliters

⅔ cup = 158 milliliters

¾ cup = 177 milliliters 1 cup = 225 milliliters

4 cups or 1 quart = 1 liter

½ gallon = 2 liters 1 gallon = 4 liters

Linear Measurements

½ in = 1½ cm

1 inch = 2½ cm

6 inches = 15 cm

8 inches = 20 cm

10 inches = 25 cm

12 inches = 30 cm

20 inches = 50 cm

CPSIA information can be obtained
at www.ICGtesting.com
Printed in the USA
BVHW060439250321
603396BV00004B/265

9 781801 726023